21st Century Skills Library

ROAD TO RECOVERY

GRIZZLY BEAR

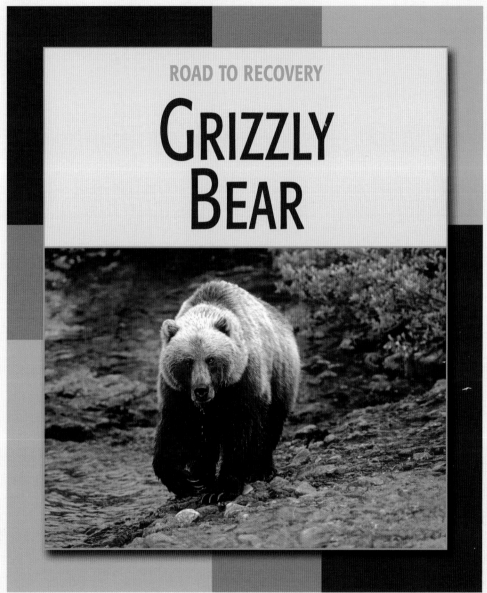

Barbara A. Somervill

Cherry Lake Publishing
Ann Arbor, Michigan

Published in the United States of America by Cherry Lake Publishing
Ann Arbor, Michigan
www.cherrylakepublishing.com

Content Adviser: Chris Morgan, Director, Grizzly Bear Outreach Project, Bellingham, Washington

Photo Credits: Cover and page 1, ©Wayne Lynch; page 4, ©Chris Morgan, www.bearinfo.org; page 7, ©AP Photo/U.S. Fish and Wildlife Service, file; pages 9, 18, and 23, ©Arco Images GmbH/Alamy; page 10, ©Cliff Keeler/Alamy; page 13, ©BRUCE COLEMAN INC./Alamy; page 14, ©Gunter Marx/Alamy; page 17, Photo courtesy of Wayne Kasworm (USFWS); page 25, ©franzfoto.com/Alamy; page 26, ©vera bogaerts, used under license from Shutterstock, Inc.; page 28, ©Catherine Lall, used under license from Shutterstock, Inc.

Map by XNR Productions Inc.

Library of Congress Cataloging-in-Publication Data
Somervill, Barbara A.
Grizzly bear / Barbara A. Somervill.
   p. cm.—(Road to recovery)
ISBN-13: 978-1-60279-315-6
ISBN-10: 1-60279-315-8
1. Grizzly bear—Juvenile literature. I. Title. II. Series.
QL737.C27S639 2009
599.784—dc22   2008024156

*Cherry Lake Publishing would like to acknowledge the work of
The Partnership for 21st Century Skills.
Please visit www.21stcenturyskills.org for more information.*

TABLE OF CONTENTS

CHAPTER ONE

THIS IS BEAR COUNTRY

Grizzly bear paws leave large tracks.

A guide points to a set of footprints in the mud. One print is oval and about 4 inches (10 centimeters) wide. It has five toes and five very large claw marks. Another print is more than 7 inches (18 cm) long. Except for the long claws, it resembles a man's footprint. The tracks tell the group that a huge grizzly bear—*Ursus arctos horribilis*—has passed this way. This is bear country.

To keep the group safe, the guide must look for signs of the grizzly. The tracks appear in dried mud. Where there is no mud, grizzlies still leave their mark. The guide will be on the lookout for bear **feces**, or scat, that appears in meadows and along the trail. Claw and teeth marks may show where bears have scratched and rubbed against trees. Hair sometimes clings to the sap exposed on tree trunks.

Bear food sources also provide signs that a bear has been in an area. Torn-up logs or tree stumps may indicate that a bear has been feeding on ants or termites.

Scientists no longer need to capture a bear—or any other **predator**—to identify animals that live in a region. They use one of the same methods that law enforcement officers use to identify victims and criminals. They analyze DNA, the unique **genetic** makeup of every living thing. Hair and scat can be tested for DNA. Scientists can then identify the animal and everything it has recently eaten. They can tell whether the animal is male or female. They can also tell if any other bears in the region are relatives.

Overturned rocks show places where bears have searched for other insects. Bushes stripped of their berries indicate that a bear has gone on a feeding frenzy. Fish parts near ponds and rivers also tell of bears in the area. And humans should beware of areas with a heavy odor of rotting meat. It may be the smell of a bear's cache. A cache is the place where a bear hides a large animal carcass for a later meal.

The guide holds up his hand to halt the hikers. A large female bear, known as a sow, and two cubs are feeding on the edge of an open meadow. The hikers must stay far

Grizzlies usually have between 1 and 3 cubs in a litter.

away from the sow. She may see people as a threat to her cubs.

It is late summer. Berries ripen in thickets at the meadow's edge. The bears feast on the sweet, ripe fruit. The cubs are 8 months old, frisky, playful, and hungry. The bond between cub and mother is strong. The cubs learn everything they need to know to survive from their mother. She teaches them where to find food, how to dig a den, and how to protect themselves.

More important, she protects them with her life. Nearly half of all cubs die in their first year. They suffer from disease, starvation, and injury. Adult grizzlies have few natural enemies, but cubs are often killed by wolves and other predators. Even male bears will sometimes try to kill a female's cubs. But female bears are devoted mothers. A female grizzly will take on a male twice her size to protect her cubs from danger. The instinct a mother has to protect her young is strong. It is nature's way of making sure the species survives.

CHAPTER TWO

THE STORY OF GRIZZLY BEARS

A grizzly bear's fur is thicker in the winter than in the summer.

Bears that live along the coast and in Alaska are generally called brown bears. Those that live inland are called grizzly bears. Brown bears and grizzly bears are not different species. They are subspecies of the family group known as *Ursus arctos,* the bear of the north. The term *grizzly* refers to the coloring of grizzly bear fur. A grizzly's hairs

A grizzly bear feeds on the remains of an elk.

are white or tan at their tips. In the lower 48 states, grizzly bears live in 5 population groups in Idaho, Montana, Wyoming, and Washington.

Grizzly bears can live in many habitats. They live in temperate rain forests, high meadows, remote mountain regions, and river valleys. Bears require territories with a variety of food throughout spring, summer, and fall. They need water and a place to den in the winter. Yellowstone has the largest bear population in the lower 48 states. There, male bears range over a territory of about 540 square miles (1,399 square kilometers). Females have smaller home ranges of about 175 square miles (453 sq km). Unlike many species, bears are not territorial. Their home ranges may overlap with other bears' ranges. In Yellowstone, for example, about 10 bears share 1,000 square miles (2,590 sq km).

Grizzly bears are omnivores. More than 80 percent of a grizzly's diet is made up of plants and insects. In early spring when they emerge from their winter dens, grizzlies eat grasses, roots, and tubers. They also feed on ants, termites, worms, and carrion.

Summer berries are a feast for grizzly bears. They have been known to gobble more than 10,000 berries in one huge meal. A slightly more unusual meal is cutworm moths. Each morning, the moths drink nectar and then

Cubs are born during hibernation, which is hard on a sow's body. Scientists have found that very large female grizzlies are more successful at birthing and raising cubs. The larger the female, the more fat she has on her body. Females with more body fat can produce more milk for their young. Larger, fatter females are more likely to produce enough milk to keep their cubs alive and healthy.

Do you think that information about food availability would be helpful to conservationists working to increase bear populations? Why or why not?

gather on hillsides. Grizzlies climb the mountains to get at these sweet, nutritious moths. They may eat between 10,000 and 20,000 moths each day.

Grizzly bears will feed on lake and river fish and on fish eggs. Most of the meat in a grizzly's diet, however, comes from moose, elk, mountain goats, and wild sheep. These animals are eaten freshly killed or as carrion. Bears will eat whatever is available.

Grizzlies are large bears. Cubs weigh only about 1 pound (0.45 kilograms) at birth. But they grow quickly on their diet of mother's rich milk. By the time they are 1 year old, they weigh about 100 pounds (45 kg). The average weight

Two grizzly bear cubs cling to their mother's back. They are between 2 and 3 months old.

for an 8-year-old adult female bear is between 250 and 350 pounds (113 and 159 kg). An average full-sized male weighs between 400 and 600 pounds (181 and 272 kg) by the time it is 12 years old. Adult grizzly bears stand about 3 feet (1 meter) tall at the shoulder and measure about 7 feet (2 m) long. But don't let their size fool you into thinking grizzlies are slow moving. They can run as fast as 35 miles per hour (56 kilometers per hour) for short distances. That's as fast as a racehorse!

CHAPTER THREE

ENDANGERED!

Bears are sometimes killed if they are believed to be a danger to humans. One way to capture and move bears without killing them is to use live bear traps.

Two hundred years ago, about 100,000 grizzly bears roamed the American West. Then, as humans moved west, they took over grizzly territory. In 1922, there were 37 grizzly bear populations in the lower 48 U.S. states. Those populations were scattered from the Rocky Mountains to the Pacific Ocean. By 1975, only 5 grizzly bear populations remained, and those population groups were in serious trouble. In that year, the

U.S. Fish and Wildlife Service listed the grizzly bear as a threatened species in the lower 48 states. If grizzly bears were going to be saved, they needed federal protection.

When the grizzly bear was listed as a threatened species, the largest population lived in the Yellowstone region, an area in northwest Wyoming, eastern Idaho, and southwest Montana. The second-largest group lived in the Northern Continental Divide area in north central Montana. The other three groups were much smaller. They were the North Cascades group in north central Washington; the Selkirk Mountains group in part of northern

Idaho, northeast Washington, and southeast British Columbia; and the Cabinet-Yaak group in northwest Montana and northern Idaho. Another area in the Bitterroot Mountains of eastern Idaho and western Montana is designated as a grizzly bear recovery zone.

At the point at which grizzly bears were listed as threatened, conservationists estimated that fewer than 1,000 grizzlies lived in the lower 48 states. Increasing the grizzly bear population would be a slow and challenging process. Grizzly sows cannot reproduce until they are 5 to 8 years old. They mate in the summer but do not give birth until late the following

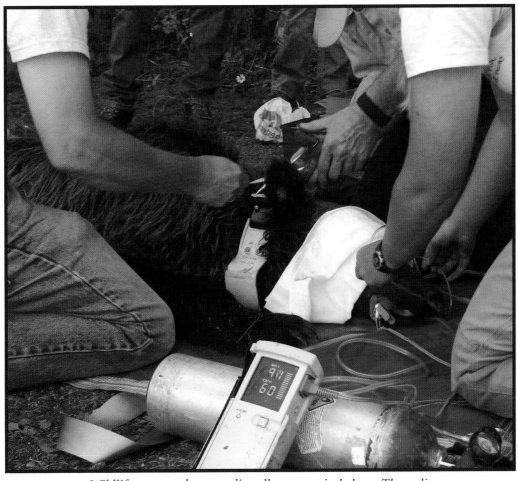

Wildlife experts place a radio collar on a grizzly bear. The radio collar will help them track the bear's movements.

winter. Sows raise their cubs for 2 to 5 years, so the cycle between one cub birth and the next could be as long as 3 years. At least half of all cubs die in their first year.

CHAPTER FOUR

THE ROAD TO RECOVERY

Bears sometimes leave clumps of fur on trees they rub against. The fur can be analyzed by scientists to help identify individual bears.

A grizzly bear recovery plan had to be created. First, scientists needed to find out how many bears lived in each population group. A bear census used to be done by counting females with cubs. Then scientists would guess how many males, immature females, and elderly bears lived in the area. Today, scientists use DNA to take an accurate bear count. Bears leave traces of themselves when they feed. They drop solid waste and snag their hair on branches and tree trunks. Scientists collect those bear traces and identify each bear that passes through an area. Cameras with special sensors are also used to help count the bears. They are placed on trails and take pictures of bears that pass by.

Grizzly bear recovery is focused on protecting habitat. Grizzlies need so much land that loss of even small amounts of habitat may cause serious bear population decreases.

Wildlife agencies have also made an effort to educate the public about grizzlies. People are taught about the proper way to store food and handle garbage when they are in grizzly territory. Bears that become used to finding

Alberta, Canada, has extended its province-wide ban on grizzly bear hunting to at least 2009. Conservationists believe that the actual number of bears in Alberta is lower than they first believed. Recent population estimates show that the province may have as few as 177 grizzlies. The Alberta government has ordered a survey to get a more accurate bear count. Counting bears is not easy. Even the best population counts require some guessing. Grizzlies spend most of their time alone. Some may be seen regularly, while others are never seen. Until the survey is completed, grizzly bear hunting will be banned in Alberta.

human food are a danger to humans. They often have to be killed to protect humans from harm.

Another area of concern for bear recovery is breeding. Each grizzly bear population group is a separate unit. That means that only bears within that group mate with one another. A small mating population can be a problem. There may not be enough **genetic diversity** in the group. Some cubs may be born with birth defects if the gene pool is too small.

One way to increase the gene pool in the low-bear-population regions is to use population **augmentation**. Population augmentation simply means adding some new animals into an already populated area. Augmenting the bear population with new bears doesn't just add to the gene pool. It can also be a way to reduce overpopulation in some areas while increasing populations in the low-bear regions.

An attempt at population augmentation occurred in the Cabinet Mountains in 1989, when bear managers estimated the population to be 15 or fewer bears. Four young females were moved into the area from British Columbia. Hair samples found 10 years later show that at least one of the released bears produced cubs. Since then, her cubs have also reproduced, making her a very successful grandmother.

Life & Career Skills

A vital part of any species recovery plan is a review of how well the plan is working. In 2007, the U.S. Fish and Wildlife Service announced a 5-year review of grizzly bears in all locations except Yellowstone. A review committee is made up of wildlife biologists, bear managers, scientists, natural resource managers, and other conservation scientists. The review will tell conservationists if the species survival plan is working or if new ideas need to be tried to help grizzlies survive.

Scientists working to save grizzly bears may also use **reintroduction**. This means placing animals into an area where no other members of their species are currently believed to be living. This might be possible in the Bitterroot region.

Adding population must be done carefully. The bears must be young, about 3 to 6 years old, and healthy. The bears being moved cannot have a history of conflict with humans, killing livestock, or rummaging through garbage. Scientists choose young bears because they adjust to their new homes more easily.

CHAPTER FIVE

A Look at Yellowstone

*Drivers must be careful in areas where bears live. Both people
and bears could be killed or badly injured in a collision.*

Grizzly bears were first listed as endangered in 1975.
Scientists developed a grizzly bear survival plan with
specific goals. The goals were different for each grizzly
bear recovery area. The rate of success for each area would
be determined by looking at several things, including the
number of breeding females.

One part of the recovery plan for Yellowstone required 15 females to have cubs each year for 6 years. The region was divided into 18 bear management units. Another goal was to have at least one sow and her cubs in at least 16 of the units.

By 2005, the Yellowstone grizzly bear population had met these goals. The average number of females with cubs in the period from 1997 to 2002 was 38. That was 23 more than the goal that had been set. During that same period, females with cubs lived in all 18 bear management units.

When the grizzly bear recovery program began in 1975, Yellowstone had only 136 grizzlies. Thirty years later,

Grizzly populations will probably never be as large as they were centuries ago. But experts are working hard to keep the bears on the road to recovery.

all goals for Yellowstone grizzly recovery had been met. The federal government announced plans to remove Yellowstone grizzlies from the endangered species list, an action known as delisting. Many people protested. They worried that the number of bears would go down again if

This sign in Kluane National Park in Canada warns visitors that they are in bear territory.

they were not protected. Some scientists still believe that it is too early to take the Yellowstone population off the endangered species list.

Other people were happy that the bears were being delisted. When grizzly bears were federally protected, hunting, logging, mining, and driving recreational vehicles in bear territory were prohibited. Housing and road projects in bear country came to a halt. Ranchers and farmers lost livestock and pets to hungry bears. Some people looked forward to being able to resume the activities that had to stop when bears were protected.

What many people don't realize is that grizzly bear protection on federal land will continue. Only bears that have spread onto private land will lose protection. But even those bears will have some legal protection. The governments of Idaho, Wyoming, and Montana are now responsible for the grizzly's continued survival. And if the bear population drops too low, grizzlies will go back on the endangered species list.

Today, more than 600 bears live in the recovery zone. Many bears have moved onto neighboring land. Yellowstone is a grizzly bear haven. Conservationists are

A grizzly bear roams in Yellowstone National Park.

continuing efforts to increase grizzly bear populations in the other recovery areas. The future looks brighter for grizzly bears now.

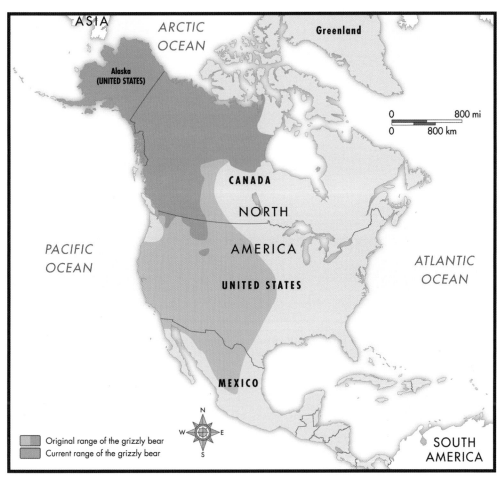

Both the light and dark green areas were once home to grizzly bears.
The dark green area shows the current range of grizzly bears.

Glossary

augmentation (awg-men-TAY-shuhn) the act of adding to or increasing something, such as a population

carrion (CAIR-ee-on) rotting flesh of a dead animal

census (SEN-suhss) an official count of the number of individuals in a population

conservation (kon-sur-VAY-shuhn) the protection of valuable things, especially forests, wildlife, and natural resources

DNA (dee-en-AY) abbreviation for deoxyribonucleic acid, the molecule that contains the genetic code for living things

endangered species (en-DAYN-jurd SPEE-sheez) a group of similar animals or plants that is in danger of dying out completely

feces (FEE-sees) the solid waste of an animal

genetic (juh-NET-ik) involving the traits or characteristics carried on genes and passed on from parents to their offspring

genetic diversity (juh-NET-ik di-VUR-suh-tee) having a wide range and variation of genes within a species

habitats (HAB-uh-tats) the places where an animal or plant naturally lives and grows

hibernation (hye-bur-NAY-shun) the act of sleeping through the winter

omnivores (OM-nuh-vorz) animals that eat both meat and plants

predator (PRED-uh-tur) an animal that hunts and eats other animals

reintroduction (ree-in-truh-DUHK-shuhn) the act of putting animals into an area where members of their species no longer exist

FOR MORE INFORMATION

Books

Greene, Jacqueline Dembar. *Grizzly Bears: Saving the Silvertip*. New York: Bearport Publishing, 2008.

Sartore, Joel. *Face to Face with Grizzlies*. Washington, DC: National Geographic, 2007.

Stevens, Kathryn. *Grizzly Bears*. Mankato, MN: The Child's World, 2008.

Web Sites

National Geographic Grizzly Bear Profile
animals.nationalgeographic.com/animals/mammals/grizzly-bear.html
For more grizzly bear facts and photos

North American Bear Center
www.bear.org/
Learn more about North American bears of all kinds

The North Cascades Grizzly Bear Outreach Project
www.bearinfo.org
Discover information about grizzly bears and the status
of the Northern Cascades population

INDEX

ABOUT THE AUTHOR

Barbara A. Somervill writes children's nonfiction books on a variety of topics. She believes that researching new and different topics makes writing every book an adventure. When she is not writing, Ms. Somervill plays duplicate bridge, reads avidly, and travels.